Popular Concert Favorites

for

Clarinet

mmo

CD 3831

MMO CD 3831
MMO Cass. 7058

Music Minus One

Popular Concert Favorites
Trumpet

Band No. Complete Version		Band No. Minus Trumpet	Page No.
1	Bach: Sarabande	13	4
	Ditterdorf: Tournament of Temperaments:		
2	The Melancholic	14	6
3	The Humble	15	6
4	The Gentle	16	7
5	Schumann: Träumerei	17	5
6	Mendelssohn: Solemn March	18	8
7	Chopin: Prelude	19	12
8	Schubert: Moment Musical	20	9
9	Bizet: Toreador Song	21	10
10	MacDowell: To A Wild Rose	22	12
11	Verdi: Triumphal March (from Aida)	23	13
12	- Tuning Notes, A440 -		

Sarabande

J. S. Bach (1685-1750)

MMO CD 3831

Träumerei

Robert Schumann (1810-1856)

MMO CD 3831

Tournament of Temperaments
1. The Melancholic

Ditters von Dittersdorf (1739-1799)

2. The Humble

MMO CD 3831

3. The Gentle

Andantino

Solemn March

Felix Mendelssohn (1809-1847)

Andante maestoso

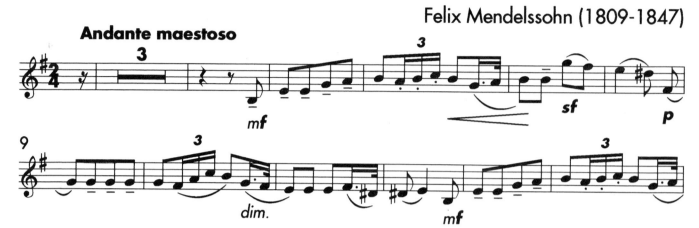

Moment musical

Franz Schubert (1797-1828)

Toreador Song

Georges Bizet (1838-1875)

To a Wild Rose

Edward MacDowell (1860-1908)

Prelude

Fryderyk Chopin (1810-1849)

Triumphal March (from *Aida*)

Giuseppe Verdi (1813-1901)

45

cresc.

49

f

53

cantabile

p

58

64

mf

69

f   mf

3

3

75

3   3   3   3

80

pp   3

85

3   f   3

90

f   3   3

Popular Concert Favorites

for Trumpet

CD 3831

MUSIC MINUS ONE 50 Executive Boulevard • Elmsford New York 10523-1325